IMMA DRUG

AND OTHER RELATED POEMS

by
Jerry Tobias

Teddy Bear Press

About the Imma Drawings

The drawings in this book portray my children, other family members, and close friends. To each of these people, I feel deeply and eternally bonded. I hope my portrayals convey these feelings to them and to my extended Imma family.

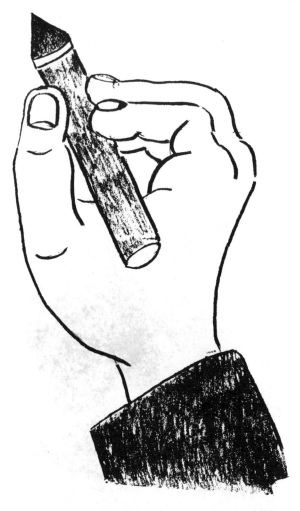

ISBN 1-880017-12-1

Table of Contents

Here are some drugs
I want you to see;
I hope that you will learn
from these examples of me.

To Pank, Big Toby, Donna Marie,
and all my children,

Imma yours.

To Barbara Toth for her
editorial guidance and consultation,

Imma yours, too.

Imma Says

Imma books
    will help you learn;
they deal with subjects
    of concern.

The verse is meaningful
    and lots of fun;
it can be understood
    by everyone.

The Imma pictures
    will educate;
they make it easy
    to communicate.

So read your Imma
    and learn from it;
you'll find the teachings
    a benefit.

Introduction

Imma drug
    that does heal;
I have great
    healing appeal.

I'm a substance
    that must be carefully used;
I'm a substance
    that must not be abused.

I'm medically prescribed
    by doctors today;
I'm prescribed by them
    to make illness go away.

But I'm sometimes misused
    by prescription users;
I call these misusers
    substance abusers.

I'm made and sold
    by drug dealers too;
they mix together
    an illegal brew.

I can hurt
    the substance abuser;
I can harm
    the illegal user.

Imma drug
    that should be inscribed,
"I should only be used
    as medically and legally prescribed."

Imma Alcohol

Imma alcohol
    or No. 1 abuser;
I can hurt
    an alcohol misuser.

I'm found in liquor,
    beer, and wine;
I'm fermented grain, cereal,
    and fruits of the vine.

I'm a colorless liquid
    that's made into drink;
I'm a substance
    that controls how misusers think.

I can tranquilize
    and stimulate too;
I control behavior
    and what a misuser can do.

I can weaken
    and cause dependence upon me;
I impair judgement
    and what a misuser can see.

I cause accidents
    and sickness too;
I cause unhappiness
    with my brew.

Imma alcohol
    that does confess,
"I can make a misuser's life
    an awful mess."

Imma Amphetamine

Imma amphetamine
with a stimulating claim;
I'm a drug
that uses *speed* for an illegal nickname.

I'm a substance
that's medically used,
but I'm a drug
that's often misused.

I can affect the health
of the misuser;
I can change the personality
of the abuser.

I cause anxiety and irritability
for the misuser;
I cause aggressiveness and sleeplessness
for the abuser.

I develop tolerance
and dependence too;
I can even cause death
for abusers who do.

Imma amphetamine
with this creed,
"Only take me as prescribed
and never mess with *speed.*"

Imma Barbiturate

Imma barbiturate
    or sedative by call;
I'm also known
    as a "sedatal."

I'm a drug
    that does good,
but I must be taken
    only as I should.

I sedate nerves
    and put them at ease;
I can help psychiatrists
    fight mental disease.

I reduce anxiety
    and tension too;
I also counteract insomnia
    with my brew.

I have the tendency
    to be misused;
I'm also able
    to be abused.

I cause problems
    for the misuser;
I cause accidents
    for the abuser.

Imma barbiturate
    with this scoop,
"Misuse me, and
    you're a nin-com-poop."

IMMA SAYS:

TOO MUCH CAFFEINE
CAN OVER STIMULATE
YOU.

DON'T ABUSE
CHOCOLATE.

Imma Chocolate

Imma chocolate
of "yum-yum" fame;
I also have
a stimulating claim.

I have caffeine
inside of me;
I use caffeine
to make my "yummy."

I'm a sweet
that's good to eat;
I'm a "yum-yum"
that's just plain sweet.

I'm brown in color
and small in size;
I'm a "yum-yum"
that's quite a prize.

I'm eaten by many
everyday;
I'm a "yum-yum"
with a tasty say.

I stimulate overusers
with my caffeine;
I can change
their metabolic scene.

Imma chocolate
with this adieu,
"If you abuse me,
I can overstimulate you."

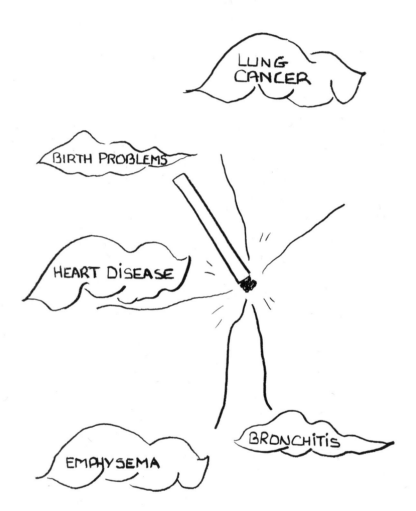

Imma Cigarette

Imma cigarette
    and stimulant too;
I have chemicals
    that can hurt you.

I have hundreds of chemicals
    inside of me;
I even have cancer agents
    in my family.

I'm four inches long
    and round about;
I appear harmless,
    but there's much doubt.

I injure the lungs
    and heart too;
I cause bronchitis and ulcers
    with my brew.

I even harm those
    who smell my smoke;
I can hurt
    the nonsmoking folk.

I'm a habit
    that's not smart;
I'm a habit
    that's dangerous to start.

Imma cigarette
    with this "smokeroo,"
"Cigarette smoking
    is not good for you."

Imma Cocaine

Imma cocaine
    and falsely named "Happy Dust";
I'm an illegal stimulant
    with a deadly thrust.

I was born in South America
    and live in Columbia today;
I travel illegally
    to the U.S.A.

I'm a white powder
    that looks like snow;
I make the nervous system
    get up and go.

I stimulate users
    with a false feeling;
I make them think
    that I'm appealing.

I create anxiety
    and a sense of doubt;
I cause restlessness
    and acting out.

I make coke users
    dependent on me;
I hook them up
    with my "Big C."

Imma cocaine
    with this important communiqué,
"If you snort me,
    you'll burn your nose away."

Imma Coffee

Imma coffee
    that contains caffeine;
I'm a member
    of the caffeine scene.

I have great
    meal appeal;
I'm often consumed
    with great zeal.

I'm a drink
    that many choose;
I'm a drink
    that many misuse.

I stimulate the misuser's
    metabolic rate;
I can create
    an active state.

I increase the pulse rate
    and heartbeat too;
I cause anxiety and irritability
    with my brew.

I confuse misusers
    and affect their concentration;
I can irritate the stomach
    with a burning sensation.

Imma coffee
    with this plea,
"It might be wise
    to decaffeinate me."

Imma Crack

Imma crack
    or smokable coke;
I'm cocaine
    that users smoke.

I'm sold in pieces
    that resemble chips;
I'm sold as pellets
    or soap-like strips.

I'm easy to get
    and inexpensive to try;
a ten dollar bill
    can make an illegal buy.

I hook the user
    with great speed;
it doesn't take long
    to establish a need.

I create
    an artificial high;
I provide a feeling
    that tends to falsify.

I can create
    a terribly violent state;
I have the ability
    to miserably agitate.

Imma crack
    that does attest,
"I can cause death
    with a cardiac arrest."

Imma Designer Drug

Imma designer drug
    which means I'm homemade;
I'm especially designed
    for today's illegal trade.

I'm designed to imitate
    illegal dope;
I modify its structure
    and its scope.

I'm derived from
    a similar compound;
I'm chemically engineered
    by the drug underground.

I can be stronger
    than what I imitate;
I have the power
    to incapacitate.

I cause physical problems
    such as nausea and chills;
I can cause fear
    and psychological ills.

Imma designer drug
    with this final line,
"I have the ability
    to create a most dangerous design."

Imma DMT

Imma DMT
    or "Dumb-Mental-Trip";
I can cause
    a mind to flip.

I'm a hallucinogen
    or psychedelic by call;
I cause disturbing hallucinations
    for one and all.

I can change
    sight and sound;
I can make things
    spin around.

I work fast
    in a moment or two;
I am quick
    to do what I do.

I'm made by illegal dealers
    and cheap to buy;
I'm always ready
    for a frightening high.

I can create tolerance
    and dependence too;
I'm considered
    a dangerous brew.

Imma DMT
    with this advice,
"If you play with me,
    you'll pay a terrible price."

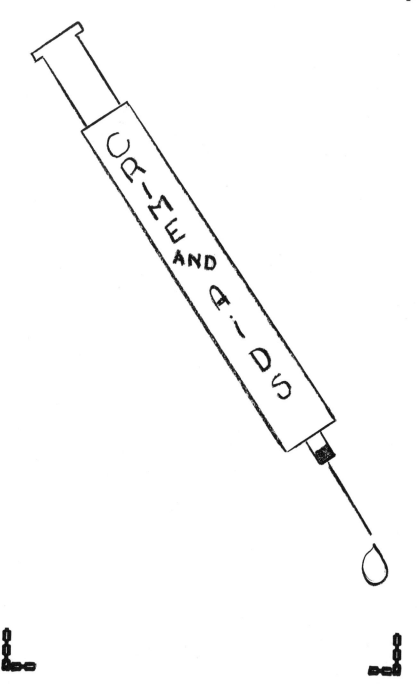

Imma Heroin

Imma heroin
 or opiate by name;
I'm known for "Smack"
 and "Horse" fame.

I'm an illegal drug
 that causes harm;
I'm the No. 1 cause
 of community alarm.

I'm used by thousands of people
 in the world today;
I'm seemingly used
 to chase frustration away.

I temporarily relieve fears
 and elevate the mood;
I create a false contentment
 and an uncaring attitude.

I start a habit
 that's horrible to kick;
I create a dependence
 that's hard to lick.

I force users
 to commit crime;
I cause health problems
 and waste valuable time.

Imma heroin
 with this high,
"If you run with me,
 it's good-bye."

Imma Ice

Imma ice
> or "Meth" by name;

I'm an illegal drug
> with a disastrous claim.

I came from Asia
> to the U.S.A.;

I settled in Honolulu
> down Hawaii way.

I provide a false feeling
> that comes on quick;

I have the ability
> to make users sick.

I can last
> for eight hours or more;

I've been known
> to last for twenty-four.

I cost fifty dollars
> for a bag of ice;

sellers sell me
> at this price.

I cause damage
> to the kidney and lung;

I psychologically
> damage the young.

Imma ice
> with this advice,

"I'm a drug
> that's not nice."

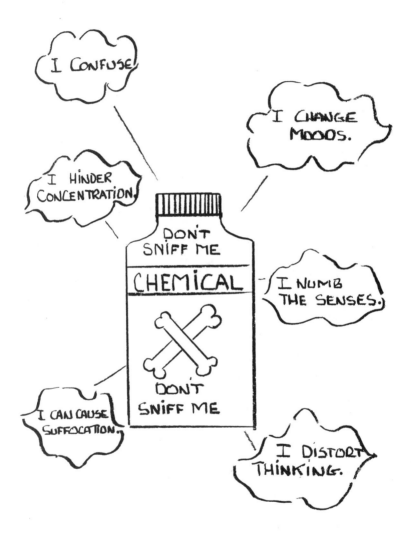

Imma Inhalant

Imma inhalant
 of sniffing fame;
I'm a breathable chemical
 with a mind-altering claim.

I'm a chemical
 that sniffers sniff;
I'm an inhalant
 with a deadly whiff.

I'm a chemical
 that's not very kind;
I can create a feeling
 that can confuse the mind.

I use young people
 for my prey;
I entice the young
 with my spray.

I change moods
 for an hour or two;
I can reduce inhibitions
 and distort thinking too.

I numb the senses
 and hinder concentration;
I can cause unconsciousness
 and suffocation.

Imma inhalant
 with this deadly tale,
"I'll hurt you
 if you inhale."

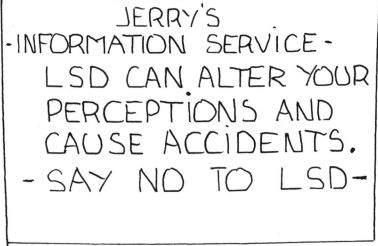

Imma LSD

Imma LSD
    or acid by call;
I can provide
    a dangerous trip for all.

I'm an illegal drug
    or psychedelic by name;
I'm best known
    for mind-altering fame.

I alter perceptions
    as never before;
I capture a mind
    for eight hours or more.

I'm taken by mouth
    and ingested quick;
it doesn't take long
    to turn my trick.

I distort senses,
    sights, and sound;
I take control
    and confound.

I confuse, depress,
    and distress;
I cause anxiety
    and restlessness.

Imma LSD
    with this adieu,
"A bad trip from me
    could be curtains for you."

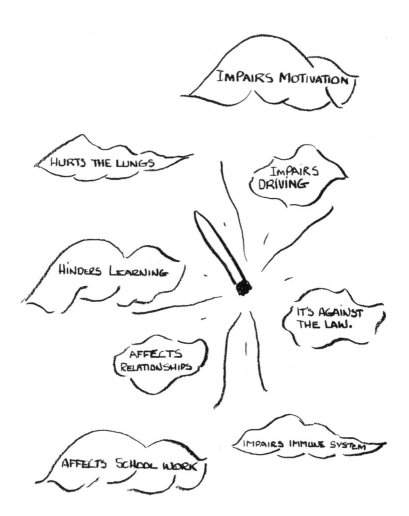

Imma Marijuana

Imma marijuana
or THC;
I'd like to tell
all about me.

I was born in Mexico
by the sea;
I came to the U.S.
in a "key."

I'm found on the flowers
of the cannabis plant;
my plant tops
can falsely enchant.

I create a false feeling
with a toke or two;
I'll burn out users
if they continue to do.

I adversely affect school
and the work users do;
I cause relationships
to suffer too.

I adversely affect the lungs
and blood pressure rate;
I cause health
to deteriorate.

Imma marijuana
with this final toke,
"I'm a drug
that's an illegal smoke."

Imma MDA

Imma MDA
    with an illegal drug claim;
"My-Drug-is-Awful"
    should be my nickname.

I come from the oil
    of a tree;
I have the power
    to cause a catastrophe.

I falsely create
    a dreamlike state;
I make it impossible
    to really communicate.

I dull the mind
    for several hours;
I can confuse
    communicating powers.

I've been known
    to wreck a relationship;
I can create
    a disastrous "communicationship."

Imma MDA
    with this communicating pill,
"I'm no substitute
    for a communicating skill."

Imma Mescaline

Imma mescaline
> or "Mesc" for short;
I'm a psychedelic
> of the hallucinogenic sort.

I'm found on the cactus
> of the peyote plant;
I'm an alkaloid
> that can falsely enchant.

I distort sounds
> and change sights;
I turn days
> into scary nights.

I'm sold illegally as powder
> or in a capsule too;
I also have
> a liquid brew.

I'm swallowed or sniffed
> by some users;
I'm sometimes injected
> by "Mesc" abusers.

I can provide
> a false appeal;
I can create
> a life that's unreal.

Imma mescaline
> with this plea,
"When it comes to mescaline,
> don't 'Mesc' with me."

METHADONE
CLINIC
DR. MADHU

Imma Methadone

Imma methadone
    with a special role;
I fight heroin
    for my goal.

I'm a substitute
    that users take;
I try to help
    make the heroin break.

I suppress the desire
    for physical need;
I have the ability
    to intercede.

I can withdraw
    or maintain the abuser;
I can stabilize
    the addicted user.

I'm taken regularly
    with a single sup;
I cost no more
    than a coffee cup.

Imma methadone
    that says for sure,
"I try real hard
    to encourage a heroin cure."

Imma "Metharest"

Imma "metharest"
  or "el-relaxo" by name;
I'm a sedative
  with a relaxing claim.

I relieve anxiety
  and tension;
I promote sleep
  and reduce apprehension.

I'm a sedative
  that can do good,
but I must be taken
  only as I should.

I've been abused
  by kids in school;
I've been misused
  to be cool.

When misused,
    I encourage foolish acts;
I confuse thinking
  and distort the facts.

I create tolerance
  and dependence too;
I adversely affect
  the things kids do.

Imma "metharest"
  that would suggest,
"Take me as prescribed
  and I'll do the rest."

Imma Mood-Altering Seed

Imma mood-altering seed
    that's not good for you;
I'm a seed
    that's a psychedelic too.

I have the ability
    to create a false high;
I've a psychoactive substance
    that can falsify.

I use my seed
    to do my work;
I use it
    to "psychedelically" perk.

I can adversely affect
    how users feel;
I can make things
    seem unreal.

I make users
    feel real bad;
I make users
    think they are mad.

Imma mood-altering seed
    that does shout,
"Don't fool with seeds
    that you know nothing about."

Imma Mood Confuser

Imma mood confuser
    that affects the mind;
I'm a plant part
    that's really not kind.

I'm made from plants
    and other substances too;
I'm used to enhance food
    and make it appealing for you.

I won't hurt
    a normal user;
I only affect
    an enhancement abuser.

I can confuse
    the abuser;
I can upset
    this type of user.

I should only be used
    for what I'm intended;
I should only be taken
    as recommended.

I should only be used
    to enhance food;
I should never be used
    to confuse a mood.

I'm a mood confuser
    with this advice,
"When I'm abused,
    I'm not very nice."

STOMACH
SETTLE

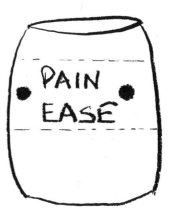

PAIN
EASE

ITCH
STOPPER

Imma Nonprescription Drug

Imma nonprescription drug
    that people buy;
I'm sold over-the-counter
    for every girl and guy.

I'm always available
    in every drugstore;
I'm placed on counters
    for consumers to explore.

I'm ready to buy
    for a dollar or two;
I try to help
    with my special brew.

I make many claims
    about what I do;
I try to live up
    to what I tell you.

I can be dangerous
    if I'm misused;
I'm a substance
    that's easily abused.

Imma nonprescription drug
    that does intervene,
"Be careful; I don't want to contribute
    to today's drug scene."

Imma Opium

Imma opium
　　　of poppy fame;
I'm made from the poppy
　　　and have a narcotic claim.

I'm made from the juice
　　　of the poppy plant;
I'm thick and gooey
　　　and can falsely enchant.

I grow in a land
　　　that's far away,
but I travel great distances
　　　to look for prey.

I carry my goo
　　　to drug marketplaces;
I look for users
　　　with wanting faces.

I sell the user
　　　my "yucky" goo;
I sell the user
　　　my destructive brew.

I sell my opium
　　　that's gooey and thick;
I sell a brew
　　　that's hard to kick.

Imma opium
　　　with this "who's whoser,"
"I come from a poppy
　　　that's a real abuser."

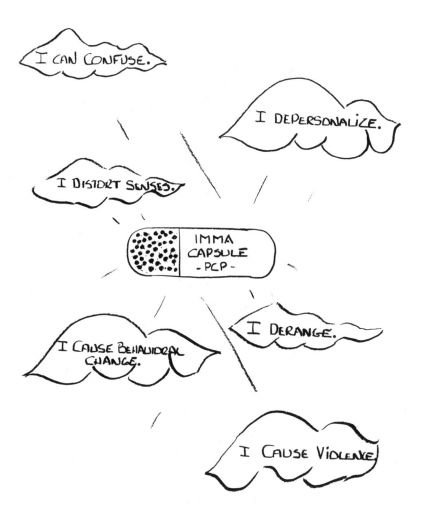

Imma PCP

Imma PCP
    or *Angel Dust* to you;
I'm an animal tranquilizer
    that's dangerous to do.

I'm hard to classify
    because of all I do;
I can concoct
    a very dangerous brew.

I'm an illegal drug
    that some choose;
I'm a powder
    with the power to confuse.

I can depersonalize
    and slow down time;
I can distort senses
    or make the user sublime.

I can cause violence
    and behavioral change;
I have the ability
    to derange.

I can last
    for twelve hours or more;
I can put a user down
    for twenty-four.

Imma PCP
    with this must,
"Don't ever experiment
    with *Angel Dust*."

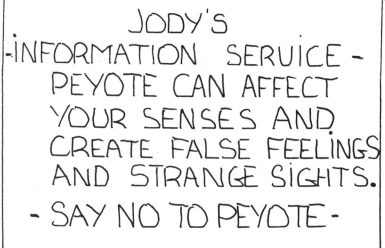

Imma Peyote

Imma peyote
of psychedelic fame;
I'm a cactus top
with a religious claim.

I'm used legally
for religious rites;
I'm supposed to provide
spiritual insights.

I'm also illegally used
by pleasure seekers;
I have "peyotists"
who are drug freakers.

I grow on cactus
in the Southwest;
I'm the top or crown
that users ingest.

I falsely create colors
and geometric lines;
I can make
confusing designs.

I create tolerance
for steady users;
I develop dependence
for peyote abusers.

Imma peyote
that would chant,
"Please don't experiment
with my cactus plant."

Imma Prescription Drug

Imma prescription drug
    or medicine for you;
I'm called "sulfas"
    and "cillens" too.

I'm prescribed by doctors
    for you to take;
I'm a prescription
    that pharmacists make.

I'm a mixture
    that's designed to cure;
I fight infection
    and temperature.

I'm specially measured
    for age and size;
I'm carefully balanced
    to individualize.

I've a dose
    with an exact amount;
I even have
    a refill count.

I must be taken
    to the letter;
it's the only way
    that users get better.

Imma prescription drug
    with this advice,
"I'm a drug
    that's quite precise."

Imma Psilocybin

Imma psilocybin
    or *Mexi-shroom* to you;
I'm a psychedelic
    that produces hallucinations too.

I was originally used
    as a religious rite;
the Aztecs used me
    as a sacramental insight.

Now I've fallen
    into illegal use;
I've become a psychedelic
    that users abuse.

I'm taken by users
    to get a false high;
I'm on the streets
    as a psychedelic buy.

I distort senses
    and change moods;
I disorient thinking
    and attitudes.

I create tolerance
    and psychological need;
I have the power
    to impede.

Imma psilocybin
    with this frightening high,
"I'm a *Mexi-shroom*
    that can terrify."

Imma Smokeless Tobacco

Imma smokeless tobacco
    or "Chaw" by name;
I also have
    a chewing tobacco claim.

I have many users
    in the U.S. today;
I have many
    that think I'm O.K.

I come in a pouch
    or a can;
I also have
    a brick plan.

I'm often chewed
    by youthful users;
I do much
    to make them losers.

I increase blood pressure
    and heart rate;
I cause gums
    to deteriorate.

I'm a suspected
    cancer producer;
I'm a threat
    to every user.

Imma smokeless tobacco
    with this flyer,
"Although I'm smokeless,
    there's plenty of fire."

Imma Soft Drink

Imma soft drink
    named Big Toby;
I'm a drink
    with caffeine in me.

I'm a drink
    that kids like;
I'm a favorite
    of "Orlando Mike."

I'm a colorful drink
    with lots of fizz;
I'm very popular
    in the soft drink biz.

I'm used by some kids
    several times a day;
I'm a drink
    with a perky say.

I'm a drink
    that's easy to find;
I'm a drink
    that can affect your mind.

I stimulate overusers
    with my caffeine;
I can create
    a moody scene.

Imma soft drink
    with this decree,
"Be aware of the caffeine
    in Big Toby."

Imma STP

Imma STP
    of "Serenity, Tranquility, and Peace" fame;
I also have
    a "Scientifically Treated Petroleum" name.

I create a false high
    and space users out;
I'm an illegal drug
    with a psychedelic clout.

I increase heart rate
    and blood pressure;
I elevate temperature
    and hyperactive measure.

I slow time
    and distort shapes;
I confuse thinking
    and create "scary scapes."

I can last
    for twelve hours or more;
I have tripped a user
    for twenty-four.

I can make
    the world seem hazy;
I make users
    think they are crazy.

Imma STP
    with this important tip,
"If you want to travel,
    I'm not the way to trip."

Imma Tranquilizer

Imma tranquilizer
or "Tranquileeze" by name;
I have
a relaxation claim.

I'm a drug
that can do good,
but I must be taken
only as I should.

I'm a drug
that's prescribed today;
I've the power
to make anxiety go away.

I relax users
and put them at ease;
I create a feeling
that tends to appease.

I'm a relaxer
that's easily misused;
I'm an appeaser
that's often abused.

I can develop
a tolerance for misusers;
I can create
a dependence for abusers.

Imma tranquilizer
with a word to the wise,
"Reduce anxiety
with physical exercise."

Imma's Favorite List

Imma's favorite list
    is made especially for you;
it offers the Imma user
    a special job to do.

It asks you to list
    your favorite poem;
Imma doesn't care
    where you roam.

It asks for a list
    that Imma can see;
it asks for a list
    of one, two, or three.

Now here is the list
    for you to fill in;
here is the list,
    so you can begin.

1. _____

2. _____

3. _____

Imma says "thanks"
    for your special assist;
you are now a maker
    of Imma's favorite list.

In Conclusion

I hope you enjoy
        my Imma book;
it's made for you
        to read and look.

I want you to know
        what drugs do;
I want you to know
        how they affect you.

A drug is a substance
        that is here to stay;
a drug is a substance
        that affects your day.

A drug touches
        every childhood;
a drug is found
        in every neighborhood.

So know your drugs
        and why they are here;
you will be much safer
        when they appear.

Imma's X Game

Find the word
that doesn't fit;
examine each row
and place an X on it.

ALERT	ALERT	ALERT	DULL
CLEAR	CLEAR	CONFUSED	CLEAR
HAPPY	UNHAPPY	HAPPY	HAPPY
HEALTHY	HEALTHY	HEALTHY	UNHEALTHY
HONEST	HONEST	DISHONEST	HONEST
INDEPENDENT	DEPENDENT	INDEPENDENT	INDEPENDENT
LEGAL	LEGAL	LEGAL	ILLEGAL
MOTIVATED	MOTIVATED	UNMOTIVATED	MOTIVATED
NORMAL	ABNORMAL	NORMAL	NORMAL
ORIENTED	ORIENTED	ORIENTED	DISORIENTED
REAL	REAL	UNREAL	REAL
RELAXED	RESTLESS	RELAXED	RELAXED
REMEMBER	REMEMBER	REMEMBER	FORGET
USE	USE	MISUSE	USE

Imma says thanks
for playing X with me;
you have helped
with Imma's "ex-ta-see."

Imma's Spelling Bee

Here are some words
      I want you to spell;
take your time
      and try to do well.

D __ CT __ R

D __ __ G

DR __ GS __ O __ E

DR __ GG __ __ T

L __ G __ L

M __ D __ CI __ E

N __ RC __ T __ C

PH __ RM __ C __ __ T

PH __ RM __ __ Y

PR __ S __ R __ BE

PR __ SC __ __ PT __ __ N

Imma says thanks
      for spelling with me;
you have helped
      with Imma's spelling bee.

The Imma Match Game

Here are some matches
that Imma made for you;
please match Imma 1
with Imma 2.

Imma 1	*Imma 2*
1 alcohol	___ prescribed by doctors
2 barbiturate	___ sold over-the-counter
3 cigarette	___ My-Drug-Is-Awful
4 DMT	___ adversely affects school work
5 inhalant	___ a dangerous trip
6 LSD	___ "I'll hurt you, if you inhale me."
7 marijuana	___ Dumb-Mental-Trip
8 MDA	___ Smoking is not good for you.
9 nonprescription drug	___ "sedatal"
10 prescription drug	___ No. 1 abuser

Now it's time
for correcting fun;
so start with 10
and count back to 1.

A Word About the Author

JERRY T.
by
DONNA T.

Dr. Tobias is a professor of Education and Human Services at the University of Detroit. He also is a practicing counselor in the community. He has a Doctorate in Education and has trained counselors and counseled local youth for the past twenty-five years. Jerry loves his work and feels that his teaching and counseling practice blend well together.

He enjoys writing for young people and has written several youth-oriented books and articles. He writes everyday and aims his verse at enriching youthful growth and development. Jerry hopes that his young readers will learn from his efforts.

Jerry has raised four children and feels that his "Imma Books" are his fifth child. He personally researches all the material and then puts it into a meaningful rhyme.

He loves his "Imma Books" and hopes to put out a series of them over the next few years.